W9-CIG-365

YOUTH WITH AGGRESSION ISSUES

Bullying and Violence

HELPING YOUTH WITH MENTAL, PHYSICAL, AND SOCIAL CHALLENGES

Title List

Youth Coping with Teen Pregnancy:
Growing Up Fast

Youth Who Are Gifted:
Integrating Talents and Intelligence

Youth with Aggression Issues:
Bullying and Violence

Youth with Alcohol and Drug Addiction:
Escape from Bondage

Youth with Asperger's Syndrome:
A Different Drummer

Youth with Bipolar Disorder: Achieving Stability

Youth with Cancer: Facing the Shadows

Youth with Conduct Disorder:
In Trouble with the World

Youth with Cultural/Language Differences:
Interpreting an Alien World

Youth with Depression and Anxiety:
Moods That Overwhelm

Youth with Eating Disorders:
When Food Is an Enemy

Youth with Gender Issues: Seeking an Identity

Youth with HIV/AIDS: Living with the Diagnosis

Youth with Impulse-Control Disorders:
On the Spur of the Moment

Youth with Juvenile Schizophrenia:
The Search for Reality

Youth with Aggression Issues

Bullying and Violence

by Kenneth McIntosh
and Ida Walker

Mason Crest Publishers
Philadelphia

Mason Crest Publishers Inc.
370 Reed Road
Broomall, Pennsylvania 19008
(866) MCP-BOOK (toll free)
www.masoncrest.com

First printing

1 2 3 4 5 6 7 8 9 10

ISBN 978-1-4222-0133-6 (series)

Library of Congress Cataloging-in-Publication Data

McIntosh, Kenneth, 1959–

  Youth with aggression issues : bullying and violence / by
Kenneth McIntosh and Ida Walker.

      p. cm. — (Helping youth with mental, physical, and
social challenges)

  Includes bibliographical references and index.

  ISBN 978-1-4222-0136-7

  1. Bullying—Juvenile literature. 2. Violence—Juvenile literature. 3. Aggressiveness—Juvenile literature. I. Walker,
Ida. II. Title.

BF637.B85M325 2008

305.235086'920973—dc22

2006038610

Interior pages produced by
Harding House Publishing Service, Inc.
www.hardinghousepages.com
Interior design by MK Bassett-Harvey.
Cover design by MK Bassett-Harvey.
Cover Illustration by Keith Rosko.
Printed in the Hashemite Kingdom of Jordan.

The creators of this book have made every effort to provide
accurate information, but it should not be used as a substitute for
the help and services of trained professionals.

Contents

Introduction

We are all people first, before anything else. Our shared humanity is more important than the impressions we give to each other by how we look, how we learn, or how we act. Each of us is worthy simply because we are all part of the human race. Though we are all different in many ways, we can celebrate our differences as well as our similarities.

In this book series, you will read about many young people with various special needs that impact their lives in different ways. The disabilities are not *who* the people are, but the disabilities are an important characteristic of each person. When we recognize that we all have differing needs, we can grow toward greater awareness and tolerance of each other. Just as important, we can learn to accept our differences.

Not all young people with a disability are the same as the persons in the stories. But you will learn from these stories how a special need impacts a young person, as well as his or her family and friends. The story will help you understand differences better and appreciate how differences make us all stronger and better.

—*Cindy Croft, M.A.Ed.*

Did you know that as many as 8 percent of teens experience anxiety or depression, and as many as 70 to 90 percent will use substances such as alcohol or illicit drugs at some time? Other young people are living with life-threatening diseases including HIV infection and cancer, as well as chronic psychiatric conditions such as bipolar disease and schizophrenia. Still other teens have the challenge of being "different" from peers because they are intellectually gifted, are from another culture, or have trouble controlling their behavior or socializing with others. All youth with challenges experience additional stresses compared to their typical peers. The good news is that there are many resources and supports available to help these young people, as well as their friends and families.

The stories contained in each book of this series also contain factual information that will enhance your own understanding of the particular condition being presented. If you or someone you know is struggling with a similar condition or experience, this series can give you important information about where and how you can get help. After reading these stories, we hope that you will be more open to the differences you encounter in your peers and more willing to get to know others who are "different."

—*Carolyn Bridgemohan, M.D.*

Chapter 1

Cain's Girl

The boy slumped against the back wall of the restaurant, moaning. His attackers had torn his shirt, pulled off his shoes, and thrown them away. One eye was already puffed shut, and his lip was swollen.

Jada tried to avert her gaze and act as if he weren't there; she pulled at the pleats of her cheerleader's skirt to straighten it, put her chin up, and looked straight ahead as she walked by. Yet she couldn't help but cast a quick guilty glance toward the injured boy. She tried to tell herself, *I'm only an innocent bystander*, but her conscience yelled in reply, *Liar*.

How much had changed in the past half year. . . .

When her mom and she moved to Huntington Beach, Jada had been delighted but apprehensive. The beach community was so much newer, brighter, and cooler than where she lived before. The kids at Shore View High dressed in the newest fashions, drove expensive cars, and in every way seemed superior to students at her old school. So Jada was happy that she and her Mom were moving up in the world, yet fearful she might not measure up to the standards of teen life in Surf City.

She tried out for cheerleading and made the squad. The other girls were aloof, however. The coach liked her, and she did well at all the routines, but it was hard to fit in. Sometimes she ate alone in the cafeteria; other times she would sit with the girls from the squad but on the edge of their group, hanging around but not with the others.

During those difficult first few weeks at Shore View, Jada asked herself, *Is it my clothes?* She made do the best she could with her meager allowance, but she knew the other kids could tell the difference between cheap boutique apparel and fashions bought in the better stores. She wondered if her skin color made a difference. Deep in her heart, she truly believed biracial women were the most beautiful in the world, and her dark skin, auburn hair, and green eyes did attract attention—but was she just kidding herself? Did people not like her because she was black? At her old school, she seemed to fit in with everyone; here she felt like an outsider to all.

Then everything changed. It started with the horrifying touch of a hand lifting the back of her skirt, squeezing her bottom. Jada spun around, her mouth open, eyes wide—but no sound came from her throat. She wondered ever since: what if she had screamed? Swore? Slapped the offender? But she was too scared to do those things. And confused.

She had been waiting for the city bus to take her home after practice when she felt the hand on her body. Startled, she spun around—and found herself looking up at Cain Williams, the, blond, muscular star of the senior basketball team.

Jada's head twirled. On the one hand, she was shocked, frightened, and angry. And at the same time, she knew how hard the other girls on the squad tried to capture Cain's attention. And he was definitely paying attention to her now.

He looked at her with a grin, as if grabbing a girl's butt was an acceptable form of greeting. "Hey there, honey, I don't think we've met before."

Jada was trying to catch her breath, sucking air in little gasps. She couldn't think of anything to say.

"Can't find the words, huh?" He laughed. "Chicks seem to be overwhelmed by my presence."

Jada's eyes widened. *This guy is so full of himself.*

"Waiting for the bus? I can drive you home. Got that new Mustang—with the custom paint and chrome wheels over there in the lot." He pointed to a mean-looking car.

Jada glanced at the car, then shook her head like an animal spying a trap.

"We could stop and have some fun on the way. Isn't it 'bout time you got some action at Shore View, huh?"

The contents of Jada's stomach suddenly started to rise into her mouth.

"You are so hot." Cain was staring at her body like a famished dog slobbering over a piece of steak.

Jada's knees turned to jelly; she sat down quickly on the bus-stop bench.

"You're going to be my girlfriend."

The statement sounded to Jada like the Godfather promising, "I'm going to make you an offer you can't refuse." She felt a twinge of foreboding at the same time that she wanted to laugh . . . and at the same time, she couldn't help but be complimented.

He swiveled on his feet and sauntered away from the bus stop toward his car. Jada felt dizzy. This was the guy everyone at Shore View wanted to be with. He was arrogant and crude—but for some reason, he liked her.

In the following weeks, Cain harassed her daily. He could be sweet—like the roses taped onto the front of her locker.

Other times he was vile—one day she found a condom in an envelope stuck in her backpack. Cain would slide up behind her, much too close for comfort, and whisper in her ear. Once he cornered her in the hallway after practice, pushed her up against the wall, and fondled her breast.

Jada hated herself for indecisiveness. Why didn't she report him to the school counselor, or a teacher? Why didn't she tell her mom? It was so confusing. She was afraid anyone she told would disbelieve her—or ask why she was complaining. Cain was popular. He was the school's star athlete, leading the basketball team in rebounds and scoring. Not only that, he had a good reputation with the surf crowd, shredding waves on the weekend. He was rich; his father was owner of the Krazy Kat Klub, where stars would come down from Hollywood to drink and dance, and tourists crowded the aisles, hoping to glimpse celebrities.

Adding to her confusion, Cain's advances offered Jada the popularity that had eluded her as a newcomer to the school. The day roses appeared on her locker, Megan Sommers, the head cheerleader, spoke to Jada for the first time.

"Hey, I hear Cain has the hots for you."

"Huh?" Jada was lost in her thoughts, trying to decide how she felt about the roses.

"Ashley says he put flowers on your locker."

"Uh, yeah."

"Wow. You are so freakin' lucky. How'd you do it?"

"Do what?"

"Oh, silly. Stop it with the modest act. How'd you get Cain to notice you?"

"I, uh . . . nothing, really. I'm not even sure I like him."

"Get out. There's girls been trying to hook up with him for years. And he chooses you." Megan smiled. "Jada, you are so totally lucky."

"Well, I'm not so sure I'm . . ." Jada's voice trailed away, but Megan didn't seem to notice.

"Doing anything after practice?"

"No, I . . . why?"

"We're going to hang out at Sandy's Pier End Café. Why don't you come with us?"

"Sure." A smile spread across Jada's face. "I'd love to."

Megan giggled. "We've always wanted to hang with you—you just seemed so standoffish."

"Huh? I didn't think anyone liked me."

"Oh, Jada. You're a riot. We always wanted to be friends. We just didn't know how to get to know you. Well come on, let's get changed and head down to the pier."

Just like that, Jada was with the in-crowd.

All because Cain Williams was pursuing her.

Jada struggled with her better judgment. There were lots of things she didn't like about Cain—and yet he was apparently her ticket to the Shore View social scene.

So she accepted a ride home next time he asked her. It wasn't as bad as she feared. He drove like ten miles an hour, bass thumping so it rattled windows as the car rolled by, waving and smiling at everyone he saw. They waved back, and Jada flashed smiles at everyone. It felt pretty good to be cruising with the school's star jock. After that, it wasn't hard to just slide into being Cain's girl.

Then a few days later, he insisted on having sex. Jada's mom was religious, and Jada had always planned on waiting for sex until she was married—but life was moving at whirlwind speed, and she had made so many compromises already. What was one more?

All the movies and songs made sex seem like the greatest thing that ever happens to anyone, but it wasn't like that. Frankly, it was disappointing. All the girls on the squad talked about how great it would be to hook up with Cain, but for Jada, the experience left her feeling empty and uneasy.

But he could be sweet to her. He always paid for meals and drinks when they were together; and if he noticed her eyeing something in a store window, he ran in and bought it for her, despite Jada's protests. He took her everywhere, a tight arm around her waist like she was some necessary part of his wardrobe.

In very short time, Jada changed from the outcast new girl to an indispensable part of the popular cliques at Shore

View High. She was the star's girl, a cheerleader, the former wallflower now a Surf City teen celebrity.

But Jada couldn't silence the alarm bells going off in her mind. She was doing all the stuff other kids envied: hanging out with the basketball team and cheerleading squad, going to all the parties, laughing aloud, and looking great—but deep in her heart, it all felt fake, like a shiny costume she was wearing that didn't really fit her. Besides, was the glittering charade worth the cost? She tried to look at Cain's good side; she grasped onto every positive thought she could muster about him; but something about him scared her.

At home, she was sullen and withdrawn from her mother. She didn't dare show this woman who had loved her so much and so well for her whole life what a shallow, compromised creature she had become.

Jada first saw Cain's dark side after the Shore View versus Downey game. Cain played well; in fact, he scored more points than in any other game of his career. Jada and the other cheerleaders yelled, waved, and leaped with all their hearts. It was close, but Downey had an exceptional team and finished seven points ahead.

Jada waited for Cain to come out of the locker room after the game. When he emerged, she could see he was furious. They got in his Mustang, and Cain smoked the tires out of the parking lot, then shot the car down the streets at breakneck speed.

"Whoa, hey—slow down!" Jada pleaded.

"What?!" Cain slammed his feet on the brakes, and the car drifted sideways down the center of the street.

Jada grabbed onto the door handle and clutched her seat belt, her breath taken by the G-forces of the sudden maneuver.

The car stopped cold in the road, and Cain glared at her. "*Don't* you *ever* tell me what to do."

Jada trembled, bit her lip, nodded.

He fired the car back up and drove on to a party at a teammate's house, got drunk, and then dragged Jada to an empty bedroom.

A few months later, Cain was walking with Jada down Main Street. They had stopped at Harbor Style Surf Shop, where Cain bought her a Toes Off the Board sweater she had seen in the window. It seemed like a nice afternoon—until Cain brushed against Jason Hughes, walking the other way. Jada noticed Jason was walking funny; he was probably stoned, a common occurrence and part of the reason Jason was not included with the in-crowd. His fashion taste—he looked like some raggedy dark scarecrow—didn't exactly blend with the popular cliques at Shore View, either.

Cain yelled over his shoulder, "Hey! Watch where you're going!"

Jason stopped and looked at them with a funny expression, then drawled, "Wa-watch it yourself, dude." Jason was definitely buzzed.

"What?!" Cain lunged forward, grabbed Jason by the arm, and dragged him into the alley between stores. He popped back out of the alley for an instant, pointed a finger at Jada, and said, "Stay!" like you would talk to a dog. Then he went back in the alley and Jada could hear ugly sounds.

A minute later, Cain reappeared—but not Jason. Cain latched his arm tightly around Jada's waist and pulled her up the street away from the alley.

"What happened?"

He shushed her. "Don't ask. None of your business."

The next time Jada saw Jason at school, he had a black eye and walked with a slight limp.

After six months as Cain's girlfriend, Jada was frightened. Everyone else saw the popular Cain—the outstanding athlete, the rich kid who bursted with confidence—but there was also the shadowy Cain, the tough guy who enjoyed picking on weaker kids. On the one hand, he was the popular star jock; on the other hand, a bully. While the in-crowd idolized Cain, the outcasts feared and loathed him. Kids on the "in" never spoke about Cain's shadowy side. Maybe they really didn't know it was there. Or maybe it was a secret everyone recognized but no one uttered, either because they feared saying something uncool, or because they dreaded what Cain might do to them.

Cain's best friends were Shawn, a dark-haired, hulking fellow who lacked Cain's wits but admired the star player slavishly, and Bret, a smaller, sophisticated kid whose tongue was as formidable as Shawn's physique. All three were on the team, and along with Jada, they were constant presences in Cain's life. She noticed that when the three boys were together, others—even other jocks—steered clear.

The beating happened the night after the Covina game. The game had been a hard and tense one, and as it drew to an end, the teams were tied, and crowds on both sides of the bleachers were on their feet screaming. Jada and the squad had yelled until their throats were sore. Then the ref called a foul on Cain; he swore at the ref and was benched. The other player made his free throw, and Covina won by three points.

After the game, Cain was in a dark mood. He drove Shawn, Bret, and Jada to a burger stand—and there, waiting at the counter for his order, was the Covina player whom Cain had fouled.

Cain didn't say anything, but his glances communicated silently with Shawn and Bret. "Stay." The single word was spoken to Jada.

Then the three boys surrounded the Covina player. They said something quietly and whisked him out the door. Jada leaned against the wall, closed her eyes, and pinched her eyelids shut to hold in the tears. After a few minutes, Cain stuck his head in the door and said, "Come on. I don't wanna eat here after all." Jada followed him outside.

As they headed for Cain's car, Jada saw the boy slumped against the back wall of the restaurant, moaning; his attackers had torn his shirt, pulled off his shoes, and beaten his face. One eye was puffed shut and his lip was swollen. She tried to avert her gaze and act as if he wasn't there; she pulled at the pleats of her cheerleader's skirt to straighten it, put her chin up, and looked straight ahead as she walked by. Yet she couldn't help but cast a quick guilty glance toward the injured boy. She tried to tell herself, *I'm only an innocent bystander*, but her conscience yelled in reply, *Liar*. How much had changed in the past half year.

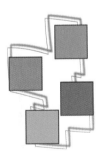

School Violence

Imagine waking up not wanting to go to school. There probably isn't a single student who hasn't lain in bed dreading going to school once in a while. Perhaps she didn't study as much as she should have for a test. Maybe he didn't get his homework done. But, for some teens, that occasional dread occurs most mornings during the school year. Why? Because these teens are the targets of violence by other teens.

Some years, stories in the media about school shootings made them seem almost commonplace. Tales of young lives lost to drive-by shootings and

Schools should be safe places where young people can learn. The threat of violence makes them sites of terror rather than education.

gang violence are all too real in the worlds of young people in some cities.

Stories such as these can lead to the impression that teen violence **pervades** North American culture today. That is not true. However, for some young people, teen-on-teen violence is very much a part of their reality—whether as victim or as victimizer.

Who Are the Aggressors?

As toddlers, many children display aggressive tendencies. One of the earliest forms of aggression is the tantrum. A young child wants something his mother

A temper tantrum is a human being's earliest form of aggression. As a child grows older, however, she will hopefully learn more appropriate ways to handle her frustration.

won't let him have. Because he has not yet learned a socially acceptable way to express his frustration and anger, the child screams, throws things, and flails his arms, hitting anyone in sight—often in full sight of strangers (and often to his parent's embarrassment). As the child matures and learns how to express that frustration, the tantrums go away, becoming just a memory. At least that's what's *supposed* to happen.

Bullying Fast Facts

- An estimated 30 percent of all U.S. teenagers are involved in bullying as either a bully, the target of a bully, or both.
- Bullying is more common among younger children and teens than among older ones.
- More boys than girls are involved in bullying, either as the bully, target, or both.
- Girls who bully are more likely to spread gossip or to encourage others to reject or exclude another girl.
- Boys are more likely to use violence in bullying.

(Source: National Youth Violence Prevention Resource Center. www.safeyouth.org)

Chapter 2
Boys Will Be Boys

Nancy Torres' shoes clicked, echoing off the empty lockers as she walked down the long hallway toward the PE office. Her fingers clenched and unclenched in nervous anticipation as she walked. She stopped in briefly at the women's faculty restroom to glance in the mirror. Yep, she told herself, everything was in place—neat and professional, just as the head counselor at Shore View High should look when about to enter into an undesired but necessary confrontation.

She left the bathroom, whisked down the hall, and knocked sharply on a door that read, "Coach James Steele."

The door swung open, and the coach stood framed in the doorway, wearing a white Shore View T-shirt and sweatpants. Stubble outlined his chin, and his hair looked like he had just come out of the shower. His face was expressionless, but his eyes narrowed on seeing the counselor.

"Hello, Coach."

"Hello, Ms. Torres. To what do I owe the honor of this visit?"

"Do we have to talk in the hallway, or are you going to invite me in?"

He stepped back from the door and made a sweeping gesture toward the chair beside his desk. Nancy Torres stepped into the small, grimy office, where the floor was piled with balls, nets, and jerseys. She glanced disapprovingly at the Dallas Cowboy Cheerleaders calendar on the wall. The two remained standing as the door swung quietly shut behind them.

Nancy sucked in a deep breath. "Coach, have you heard about what happened after the Covina game?"

"The boys did some partying—they were pretty discouraged. I'm sure you can understand their need to blow off some tension."

"That's not what I'm talking about."

"Well, obviously you have something on your mind, Ms. Torres, so why don't you just get right to the point? I'm a busy man. I don't get paid to push pencils around, like some people at Shore View do."

She inhaled, told herself to be calm, not to react to his childish insinuation. She got to the point. "There was a boy from the Covina team who ran into Cain Williams after the game at a restaurant, along with two of Cain's teammates. The Covina boy didn't know their names, but he said they were also basketball players."

She looked carefully at the coach's face; he betrayed no hint of any emotion or reaction. Nancy resumed, "The three of them beat the boy up, humiliated him, left him with bruises and cuts. His shirt was torn, and his shoes were missing. His parents have filed a police report, and the Covina High principal called our principal, wanting to know what we're going to do."

Coach Steele shrugged. "Jumping to conclusions, aren't we counselor? I mean, first of all, we don't know for sure that it was Cain who did this—all you have is the word of one disgruntled player on the other team. How do you know this whole thing isn't all trumped up? This could be a trick to get our star player into trouble."

The counselor felt anger swelling up in her gut. "I don't think the victim's family would file a police report if nothing happened, and the principal over in Covina seemed pretty clear about the facts."

Steele snorted. "I don't trust school bureaucrats—bunch of wusses. I'll talk to the team, though—get to the bottom of this, and let you know what I find out."

Nancy could feel her face reddening. "Darn it, Steele, why are you playing games with me? You know Cain is a bully. He picks on kids. He's mean—has no morals at all. You're just defending him because he's your star. If he were any other kid, you'd kick him off the team tomorrow."

The coach shook his head. "Now, Ms. Torres, let's not lose our composure, and let's not be accusing one another. You're new here, and I've noticed that new counselors tend to over-react. Cain is, after all, a growing young man. He can be a little rough around the edges. None of us were perfect at that age, were we?"

Nancy glared at him, dumbfounded.

Coach Steele continued, "Like I said, I will talk to the team. I'll bet this whole incident has been exaggerated, though. I suppose your head is filled with all that fancy political correctness they teach at college nowadays, but remember, Ms. Torres, boys will be boys."

"Yes, Coach," she replied in an icy voice. "Boys will be boys, and bullies will be bullies. That's why we're developing a comprehensive policy about student violence. I don't care if he is your pet, I'll be watching Cain Williams—and if he victimizes other students, I will see he receives the proper consequences."

"Yeah, missy, you do what you've gotta do." The coach gave her a wink. "Now I've got lots of things to attend to, so I believe this little chat is finished."

Without another word, she pivoted on her heels and strode out the door.

Heading back to the office, Nancy Torres' mind was a swirl. *He's coddling a violent young man, and Cain Williams has got to be stopped before more people get hurt.*

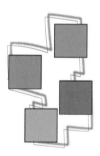

Some children never learn how to control their **antisocial** behaviors, carrying them into adolescence and adulthood. According to the National Association of School Psychologists, "childhood aggression is often viewed as an indication of a broader syndrome, frequently involving oppositional and defiant behavior toward adults and **covert** rule-breaking behaviors. These behaviors could lead to more serious and recurrent violations in adolescence, such as stealing, vandalism, assault, and substance abuse."

Who Becomes a Violent Youth?

It is impossible to tell with certainty which child will commit violent acts. There are simply too many **variables** to make that possible. Experts have, however, come up with some characteristics shared by many children who become violent. They include:

- Being socially withdrawn. Troubled children often withdraw from those around them. This withdrawal can stem from depression as well as from feelings of rejection, unworthiness, and a lack of confidence. Although most children who feel (and are) isolated are not violent, it can be the sign of a youth who has not learned how to interact with others.

- Facing repeated rejections. The key word in this characteristic is *repeated*, as everyone is rejected at one time or another. But, for the child who is repeatedly rejected—or even

A child who frequently feels isolated or rejected may turn to violence.

simply *believes* she is being rejected—these rejections can lead to increased feelings of hostility. How a child reacts to such a situation depends on the support system.

- Being a victim of violence. It's almost common knowledge: violence breeds violence. A child who grows up in a violent atmosphere has a greater possibility of becoming violent. After all, since the child faces that violence on a daily basis, he or she will likely come to believe that is "normal" behavior. Those around a child are his or her most influential teachers. If they behave in a violent manner, or **condone** violence, that message is sent to the child.

- Being picked on. During the media accounts of many acts of violence committed by teens, someone usually says that the perpetrator was picked on, teased, made fun of; in other words, he or she was not a member of the popular crowd. Though some people may think it's just a cliché or an attempt to make an excuse for the teen and his actions, according to many experts, such treatment by one's peers can lead to violence. The bullying does not always occur at school. Some youth who are harassed at home may act out violently elsewhere, especially toward someone (or some thing, such as a pet) unable to protect himself.

- Expressing violence in writings or drawings. At some point in our lives, many of us have written in a blog or diary something like, "I am just so mad at her. I'd like to . . ." and inserted some act of violence we'd like to commit against that person. Others have drawn pictures showing what they'd like to do to someone. For most, this anger is fleeting and the feelings are dealt with in nonviolent ways. Others, however, continue to exhibit their anger through increasingly violent words or images. When the verbal or visual imagery continues for an extended time, or is directed at a specific individual or group, it becomes a matter that should be looked into by a professional. Though harmless by themselves, the words and pictures can indicate that someone may be preparing to commit a violent act.

- Being prejudiced. Most people who are prejudiced are not violent. However, when

Stages of Frustration

- *anxiety*
- *stress*
- *defensiveness*
- *physical aggression*
- *tension reduction*

(Source: ERIC Clearinghouse on Disabilities and Gifted Education, 1998)

Violence breeds violence. A young person who has been abused is more likely to abuse others.

this attitude toward others mixes with other factors, such as being picked on, it can lead to violent attacks on the objects of the youth's prejudice. Membership in hate groups or visiting the online Web sites of such organizations are also signs that prejudice might be moving toward physical violence.

• Abusing drugs or alcohol. Youth who are abusing drugs or alcohol are already showing at-risk behaviors. More important in the context of committing violent acts, self-control is hindered when someone takes drugs or drinks alcohol. When sober, the youth might have been able to control his violent actions, but when under the influence of these substances, that self-control may be gone or, at least, compromised.

Chapter 3

~~~~~~

Evolution

*S*ometimes, Jada mused, *words have more than one meaning.* A discussion could take place on two entirely different levels. That seemed to be the case in Mr. Vallencio's third-period biology class.

Mr. Vallencio was short, with a white beard, mustache, and glasses; students jokingly referred to him as "the garden gnome." But they would never kid the teacher to his face—and not because of fear but because of respect. Mr. Vallencio was an educator who really understood his subject and truly cared about students. While they regularly complained, "You're giving us too much work—we have other classes too, you know," most Shore View students agreed that Mr. V. was a great guy.

At the beginning of class, Mr. V. had scrawled on the board, "Evolution: Competition or Cooperation?" Now, conversation between teacher and class was in full swing.

"So," Mr. Vallencio said, "that's Darwin's original thesis; it's all a struggle, with the roughest, toughest, smartest critters clambering over the weaker, slower, dumber ones. 'Survival of the fittest' as they say. On the other hand, we have this more recent model of evolutionary development that turns the whole thing completely on its head. It's not a matter of ruthless competition but rather of cooperation. According to the new view, natural selection is a matter of creatures working together, and those that learn to be most helpful to one another, most cooperative, ultimately survive better. So class, what do you think? Cooperation or competition?"

Josh Bruner put up his hand. "Mr. Vallencio, I hate to sound like a broken record but aren't you leaving out the other choice? What if an intelligent being designed the whole world—plants, animals, even humans—and created them just as he wanted them? There's lots of evidence for that too, and it seems simpler than either option you just presented."

Jada was still trying to understand Josh; was he a surfer posing as an intellectual, or an intellectual posing as a surfer?

Mr. V. smiled wryly. "Thank you again, Mr. Bruner, for reminding us that religion has its place at the great table of ideas. However, we've gone over this before, and I'd prefer to keep this discussion on track, if we may. So again, what do you students think if you have to pick one or the other idea—is evolution the result of competition or cooperation?"

Cain put his hand up and Mr. V. nodded at him. "Yes, Mr. Williams?"

"The new idea is just because scientists are geeks, not athletes. Look at the real world. The badder you are, the better. Tough people survive, wusses get tramped on. That's the way it is."

"Thank you for joining the discussion," Mr. Vallencio replied, "but I'm not sure you've proven your point. For one thing, I'm not convinced that the 'bad people' are the ones who ultimately do the best in life. And from a more logical perspective, does 'bad' equal competitive, Mr. Williams? Aren't you making a value judgment, bringing in morals and religion, in a different way from Mr. Bruner?" Cain looked confused, and Mr. V. turned to the rest of the class. "Are there any other thoughts on this?"

Something was rising up inside of Jada. She felt shaky and confused, but like lava rising to the top of a volcano, her emotions welled up within her until they seemed to physically push her arm into the air.

"Well, Miss Warren, nice to have you join the discussion. What do you think?"

Jada gulped, tried to choke back the words, but they tumbled out of her mouth like an eruption.

"I . . . I . . . I disagree with that. With . . . what Cain just said." She couldn't believe herself; was that her voice speaking? This was suicide. But her tongue seemed to have gained a defiant life of its own. "Survival of the fittest works in some cases, like in wars or . . . certain sports . . . but look at ants, for instance, they're little tiny defenseless things but they work together like armies to survive. Or look at how fish and dolphins work in schools. There are lots of animals that survive because they work together as a herd. Lone creatures, or animals that don't blend in well, they're the ones that become prey. Or . . . look at people. It's the thinkers, working together, who create technology and all the good stuff that helps us to live better. So it is survival of the most cooperative—not just the toughest creatures, that enable life to evolve."

Mr. V. smiled. "Bravo, Miss Warren. Well put."

But Jada barely heard the teacher's kind words. She could feel Cain's glare, his eyes boring into her. *What have I done?* She shivered, suddenly cold.

She didn't have to wait long to find out Cain's reaction. When the bell rang, normally, Jada would wait for Cain to come alongside her and escort her out the door, but this time she ran straight for her locker. Unfortunately, her locker happened to be in a little arm of the hallway off the main corridor. She was alone, her fingers shaking as she tried to open the lock, when she felt Cain's big hand squeeze her arm painfully.

"What was that all about?"

"What was what about?"

"Don't play dumb with me." His tone froze the blood in her veins. "You contradicted me in there."

"Cain, it was a class discussion, we're supposed to disagree with each other. That's how you get good grades." Her voice shook, despite the apparent truth of her words.

He repeated himself, slowly, his voice cold as steel. "You contradicted me. You made me look stupid."

"I . . . I was just talking about evolution."

"Bull."

"Cain . . . cut it out, you're scaring me."

WHAP!

He slapped her with brutal force that brought tears to her eyes.

"Don't you ever do that again." Then, even more awful than the slap, he shoved his lips onto hers and pulled their bodies together, then released her and strode away.

Jada put a hand against the locker to steady herself and fought for self-control. She wanted to cry, to puke—but she had only minutes before her next class; this was no time to let go of her emotions.

She daubed her eyes with a sleeve, drying the tears, and as her vision cleared, she spied a figure at the end of the hallway, dressed in a smart pink outfit. "Vanna, how long have you been there?"

"Long enough to see what happened."

Jada looked down at the floor, ashamed.

Vanna Khan was one of the most fashionable and popular girls at Shore View, though she didn't hang with Jada's cheerleader crowd. The rich Asian girl looked at Jada quietly for a moment. Was she going to make fun of her? No, she could see sympathy in the girl's eyes.

"Why do you put up with that?"

"He . . . he can be nice. He's not always like that."

Vanna took a few steps closer, her high heels clicking on the tiles. She dropped her voice to a whisper. "Jada, you've got looks, brains. Between the two of us, girl, you deserve better than him."

Jada was too full of confused thoughts to answer. The bell rang, and Vanna whisked away to class.

Jada stood alone, closed her eyes, and breathed deeply. *Could I do better? No one paid attention to me before Cain did. He's awful—a monster—but all the jocks and cheerleaders are on his side. If I leave him, I'll be nobody again. And. . .* Her mind flashed back to the Covina boy, bloody and slumped against the wall; and in her imagination his form changed to that of a dark-skinned girl in a cheerleader's outfit.

Herself.

Fast Facts About Aggression

- Homicide is the most common cause of death for young African American males and females.

- The intensity of aggression involving children and youth has escalated dramatically.

- Children are becoming involved in aggression at ever-younger ages.

- The United States has the highest homicide rate of any Western industrialized country, with more than 25,000 Americans murdered each year.

- Many youth in urban communities in the United States are exposed to aggression as part of their everyday life situation. In a recent study completed by NYU Child Study Center investigators, 84 percent of elementary school-age inner-city boys had heard guns being shot, 87 percent had seen someone arrested, and 25 percent had seen someone get killed.

(*Source:* NYU Child Study Center, www.aboutourkids. org)

Types of Bullying

- Cyber bullying—Using e-mail, instant messaging, Internet chat rooms, and cell phones to spread hurtful images and/or messages.

- Emotional bullying—Isolating or excluding a child from activities or spreading rumors.
- Physical bullying—Hitting, biting, kicking, and threatening physical harm.
- Racist bullying—Using racial slurs, offensive gestures, or making jokes about a child's cultural traditions.
- Sexual bullying—Making unwanted physical contact or sexually abusive or inappropriate comments.
- Verbal bullying—Name-calling, **incessant** mocking, and laughing at a child's expense.

(*Source:* www.KidsHealth.com)

A Bullying Quiz

Which of these are examples of bullying:

(a) picking on someone
(b) teasing someone
(c) insulting someone
(d) hitting someone
(e) throwing things at someone
(f) all of the above

Answer: f.

Warning Signs of Imminent Violence

The following may be indications that a youth is close to committing a violent act against himself or toward someone else:

- serious physical fighting with peers or family members
- severe destruction of property
- severe rage for seemingly minor reasons
- detailed threats of lethal violence
- possession and/or use of firearms and other weapons
- other self-injurious behaviors or threats of suicide

Immediate action should be taken by authorities when a youth:

1. has a detailed plan (time, place, method) to harm or kill others, particularly if the child has a history of aggression or has attempted to carry out threats in the past.

2. is carrying a weapon, particularly a firearm, and has threatened to use it.

(*Source:* www.utsystem.edu/pol/violence.html)

Sports act as an antidote against violence. They give young people a chance to channel their energies while offering opportunities that build a sense of belonging and achievement.

What Can Teens Do to Prevent Aggression and Violence?

- Respect others and value differences; do not bully, tease, spread gossip about others, or threaten others in any way.

- Get involved in your school and community through sports, music classes or courses, after-school programs, religious groups, or volunteering.

- Talk with an adult such as a parent or other family member, counselor, teacher, or coach if you are sad, depressed, fearful, anxious, or angry. Ask for advice if you are having trouble paying attention at school or are getting into arguments.

- Avoid alcohol and drugs.

- Learn ways to deal with disagreements without resorting to aggression, using techniques such as conflict resolution.

- Do not carry weapons.

- Report anyone planning to hurt someone to a trusted adult.

- Join efforts to stop violence in your school or community or start your own program.

(*Source:* National Youth Violence Prevention Resource Center. www.safeyouth.org)

Chapter 4
Prey

Nancy Torres sipped at her coffee, now more lukewarm than hot. She stared at the pictures of her husband and baby on the desk, then at her diploma on the wall. She had begun this job with such high hopes, thinking of all the students she could help steer down a positive path. She hadn't figured on problems with other staff members, like her conflict with Coach Steele. Nor had she realized how overwhelming kids' problems could be: unwanted pregnancy, drug addictions, depression—every student who entered her office came with a mountainous pile of problems.

Her thoughts were interrupted by a knock on the door. "Come in."

Mrs. Pao, the security guard, came through the door. "Ms. Torres, I found Jason Hughes in the hallway outside the gym. He's supposed to be in PE class now, but when I tried to get him, there he became agitated. He won't talk to me, and I don't know what to do with him, so . . ."

"Thank you, Mrs. Pao, you brought him to the right place. Jason, come in and have a seat."

The security guard left, closing the door. Jason Hughes, a gaunt dark-haired figure in faded black jeans and T-shirt, stared at the floor.

"Something wrong, Jason?"

Silence.

"Is there a reason you don't want to go to class?"

More silence.

Nancy thought for a moment. *I need to establish some rapport here.* "I see your band has been playing around town a lot, lately."

The boy glanced up at her, nodded.

"Think you've got a start on a music career?"

"Yeah, I hope so. The band feels pretty good right now."

Ah, we've got the beginning of a discussion.

"How's your mom doing?" They had talked about Jason's home life before.

"She's still a mess—but she's going to AA meetings. I guess that helps some."

"Good for her. That takes a lot of courage. How are you doing in your classes?"

"Not great—academics aren't my thing—but I am passing everything."

"Good." *Time to try to get back to the morning's problem.* "So, Mrs. Pao says you didn't want to go to PE?"

"No way I'm going."

"Some reason for that?"

Jason closed his eyes and took a breath.

"Jason, what are you avoiding in PE class?"

His eyes still closed, Jason spoke quietly, reluctantly. "It's bad in that class."

"What's bad, Jason?"

"Hassling."

"The other kids are hassling you?"

"Yeah, well . . . basically one kid."

Mrs. Torres took a guess, "I don't suppose that one kid would be Cain Williams?"

Jason opened his eyes, looked right at her. "How did you know?"

"Just guessed. What is he doing to you?"

Jason winced, looked back at the floor.

"Jason, I want to help you—and other students who Cain might be troubling. Please, help yourself—help me. What's going on?"

"Just . . . stuff. Last week when I left my locker open for a minute, he took all my street clothes and threw them in the john. I had to wait for a buddy to run to my house and get me another pair of pants and a shirt. I hid in the locker room for a whole hour. Totally sucked. And then . . ." Jason paused a moment, sighed, and resumed. "In the showers . . . he . . . snaps at me with a wet towel. I'm sick of it."

I wish there was a male counselor for this talk, Nancy thought, but there wasn't. She had to probe and get to the bottom of this. "Where does he hit you with the towel?"

Silence.

"Your genitals?"

Jason nodded, his eyes on the floor.

"That's gotta be awful humiliating."

Jason glanced up at her. "I feel like scum."

"He's hurting you emotionally as well as physically?"

Jason's voice sounded like a ghost's. "The physical pain is nothing. But . . ." He shrugged. "I totally hate school. Mostly 'cause of Cain."

"Why do you think he picks you as a target?"

Jason shrugged again. "I'm not the violent type, you know? And I'm not a jock. I guess he thinks I'm an easy target—I sort of stand out from the crowd, so I *am* an easy target. I don't know what to do."

"You shouldn't have to defend yourself in school," Nancy said. "Even if you were a fighter, that isn't your job. It's our responsibility—the staff and administration—to make sure this kind of thing doesn't go on. You don't have to take that."

Jason looked up again. "Don't do anything." He hesitated. "I'm scared."

"You're afraid of what else he might do?"

"Yeah. He can . . . he can be pretty violent."

"You've had other incidents with him?"

"Yeah, a few months ago, downtown. I . . . I wasn't feeling very good, and I sort of bumped into him on the sidewalk. He was with his girlfriend, Jada. He pulled me right into an alley and . . ."

"He hit you?"

"Beat the stuffing out of me. Hurt for weeks."

"Did you file a police report?"

"Nah. My mom, stuff going on at home, you know. I didn't want any attention from the cops, you understand?"

The counselor nodded. "Jason, you don't have to put up with this. We can stop it, right now. I'll talk to the principal, and we'll deal with Cain Williams."

"Oh, no." The boy looked panicked. "I'll be in deep trouble if you do that."

"We'll deal with Cain. I don't think he'll bother you."

"It's not just him."

Nancy tried to probe gently to get to the root of Jason's fears. "What else is it, Jason? What are you afraid of?"

"Coach Steele."

"What about Coach Steele?"

"I . . . I tried to tell him once. Told him about the trouble with Cain. Then Coach shut the door, and he said . . ."

"Yes?"

"Well, he like threatened me. Told me Cain is the school's star player, and how important the school's standing in sports was, and how if I cared about the school I wouldn't go making accusations about Cain. Told me to shut up and be a good sport, if I was smart. It was like . . . like he didn't care if I got hurt. He's protecting Cain. He didn't even care about me."

The counselor clenched her fist. "That was wrong of him, Jason. Listen, Jason, I'm going right to the principal's office to deal with this. I'll see to it that you don't get any more mistreatment—from Cain Williams or Mr. Steele."

He looked at her, unconvinced.

"Jason, would you like me to switch your schedule so you can take PE from Ms. Rice?"

He nodded vigorously.

"We might have to change a few other classes to do that."

"That's fine."

"Okay, that's what we'll do then."

Nancy turned to pull Jason's file from a cabinet, but her mind was elsewhere. She had tried talking with Cain

Williams, but he was completely uncooperative—and dishonest. He simply blamed others or claimed they were lying. It was time for action, even if she kicked open a hornet's nest doing so. She knew the principal would be behind her; he had spoken several times lately about "zero tolerance" for bullying and violence at the school. She'd let the principal deal with Coach Steele.

Nancy wondered about Cain's girlfriend, Jada Warren. What kind of issues did she struggle with? Perhaps Nancy should call her in for a chat.

It was going to be a long, difficult week.

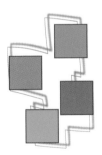

Violence Symptoms

According to the Commission for the Prevention of Youth Violence, youth who demonstrate any of the following characteristics should be referred to a mental health professional for a consultation:

- frequent loss of temper
- frequent physical fighting
- significant vandalism or property damage
- making serious threats
- extreme impulsiveness
- alcohol and other drug abuse
- easily frustrated
- hurting animals
- preoccupation with violent or morbid themes or fantasies in schoolwork, artwork, or choice of entertainment
- carrying a weapon
- name calling, use of abusive language
- **truancy**
- excessive feelings of rejection, isolation, or persecution
- gang affiliation
- feelings of depression or despair
- low self-esteem
- threatening or attempting suicide
- extreme mood swings
- deteriorating school performance

All teens are moody. Emotional ups-and-downs are part of
an adolescent's normal life, thanks to the surges of hormones
flowing through his body. When feelings of anger, depression,
or frustration become frequent and extreme, however, they may
indicate that the young person could erupt into violence.

- being witness to or the subject of domestic abuse
- setting fires
- preoccupation with weapons and explosive devices
- history of discipline problems
- social withdrawal
- blaming others for difficulties and problems

Truancy and substance abuse can be warning signs for violence.

The U.S. Surgeon General's Report on Youth Violence provides a list of risk factors that can be used to anticipate the onset, continuity, or escalation of violence in children and early adolescents:

- general offenses
- physical violence
- substance use
- being male
- aggression (among males)
- hyperactivity, restlessness
- difficulty concentrating (among males)
- risk taking
- crimes against people
- antisocial behavior
- exposure to violence on television
- medical or physical condition
- low IQ
- dishonesty (among males)

Girls and Violence

Sugar and spice
and everything nice
That's what little girls are made of.

Well, perhaps not all of them.

Identifying a male bully can be pretty easy—especially because of how he bullies, which has been discussed elsewhere. Female bullies can be much more difficult to pinpoint. According to the National

Crime Prevention Council, the girl bully "is popular, well-liked by adults, does well in school, and can even be friends with the girls she bullies." Although some girls who bully do use physical violence, the typical girl bully does not. She uses words, especially gossip and **innuendo,** to bully others. Teasing about things most teens are concerned about—hair, weight, and intelligence—is a favorite bullying method for girls. Girls who bully are also more likely to do so in groups rather than when alone with the target, and she encourages others to join her in the behavior.

Girls are not immune to physical violence, but they are more often the victim rather than the perp. When girls exhibit extremely violent behavior, it is likely to catch the attention of the press, who might give it more coverage because of its unusualness. This additional attention may make it appear as though there are significantly higher numbers of violent attacks by girls than there actually are—not completely unlike the perception of school shootings.

Dating Violence

One of the least reported areas of violence surrounds dating violence. According to the Dating Violence Resource Center (www.ncvc.org/dvrc), dating violence involves "the controlling, abusive, and aggressive behavior in a romantic relationship." The romantic relationship can be either heterosexual or homosexual.

According to a 2000 study, one in five high school girls have been hit by a boyfriend; 12 percent of male and female high school students report they had experienced some form of dating violence. Even if they were not involved in a violent relationship themselves, 40 percent of girls between ages fourteen and seventeen know someone their age who has been hit by a boyfriend. Among high school students, one in three dating relationships involves physical aggression. The highest incidence of dating violence is reported by women between the ages of sixteen and twenty-four. As the relationship intensifies, so does the violence.

Why do people stay in violent relationships? For the same reasons women have stayed in abusive marriages: embarrassment, lack of alternatives, religion, love, isolation from friends, fear.

Treating victims of dating violence can be very difficult. Besides the problems inherent in a nondating bullying situation, there is the added pressure of it being a romantic relationship. Unlike the more traditional bullying or aggressive situation, dating violence is all tied up in conflicting emotions—love for the perpetrator, fear of getting assaulted, and fear of what would happen if the relationship were terminated. There is also the peer pressure to be in a relationship. It's a lot to handle, and the victims of dating violence need to be able to find an adult they can trust, and who can help them find the strength they need not only to end the abusive relationship, but also to discover what constitutes a healthy romantic partnership.

Chapter 5
Cain's Plan

Jada felt the hard lump in her handbag and shivered. She would be less afraid if it were a snake, or even a bomb. The heavy object would soon force her to make a life-changing decision, one that could ruin her happiness whichever way it went.

After the slap, things had returned to normal for the next few days—but the trouble with normal was it kept getting worse. Jada realized she was Cain's puppet; he was kind to her only for the sake of his own pleasures. He didn't really understand her, didn't even see her as a real person. Jada was like a trophy on his shelf.

She began to see how racist he was. He'd rant about Mexicans, Asians, and blacks. She wanted to say, "What about me? I'm biracial—so why do you care about me?" But she didn't say it, because she realized with dreadful clarity that Cain didn't care about her. *My dark skin is part of why he chose me. He thinks I'm beneath him, a toy to play with and eventually discard. Because he thinks I'm inferior, he's comfortable mistreating me. I'm nobody.*

She wanted to stand up, talk back, and give him the big "we're over" speech. But she was too scared. Her popularity, her place on the squad, even her physical safety—she dared not risk it all. A thousand times a day she told herself to be quiet, go along with his wishes, and keep her hold on popularity and safety—and a thousand times a day, another part of her told her to walk away from him. She felt as though she had two minds living inside of her head—and neither of them were happy.

When Cain was expelled from school for a week, Jada didn't dare ask Cain what had happened, but she learned all about it from the gossip at school. Apparently, it had something to do with Jason Hughes, the burnout that Cain had beaten up in the alley off Main Street. Cain had been bullying Jason in PE, Jason told the counselor, and so Cain was expelled. Worse, he would miss a game when Shore View might make the championship.

And then two days after his expulsion, Cain asked Jada to do the unthinkable. They were sitting in his Mustang, parked at a bluff overlooking the ocean. In the water far below, Jada could see the white lines of surf peeling from one horizon to the other, swimmers popping up on the waves, children playing in the water's edge, and people eating sandwiches on their blankets far below where she sat with Cain. It all looked so peaceful. And so far away.

"Listen, babe, you're gonna do something for me." Cain was simmering with anger, the way he had been since getting suspended. "That jerk, Jason. It's all his fault. Stupid little stoner screwed with my life, and now he has to pay."

Jada averted her eyes from Cain's gaze; she wasn't sure what was coming next, but she was afraid of finding out.

He went on, "Everybody's watching me now, the teachers, the principal, even my parents, so you have to help me. You're still a goody two-shoes; they don't talk crap about you like they talk about me. Liars."

He reached under the seat. What was under there, she wondered.

"Jerks like Jason can't be reasoned with. His brain's too fried to make any sense, or maybe he was born messed up because of that drunk mother he has. Or maybe he's just a moron because he's part Jewish or something. Anyway, there's something not right about him." Cain found what he was looking for under the seat and sat back up, something small and shiny cupped in his hands. "So no more playing around. The little idiot has had his fun, now it's my turn. And here's how you're gonna help me. Carry this in your handbag."

He tossed a steel object into Jada's lap. She screamed, brushed it off her lap like it would bite her. Cain laughed and picked it up, grabbed Jada's hand, and pressed the cold metal against her palm. "Hold it, dummy."

Jada reluctantly gripped the gun.

"Now, here's the plan. Sooner or later—and I think it will be sooner—we're going to run into that crap-head Jason. I'll start in on him—but not real serious, kinda play with him and get his confidence up so he can take a swing or two. That way later on I can plead it was self-defense. And then, babe, when I yell, you pull that lovely little Magnum out of your purse, throw it to me, and—KAPOW!—that smack-head Jason is history."

Jada stared at the grin on Cain's face. He put his hand over hers, squeezing her fingers around the gun, then placed her hand into her purse. The revolver dropped to the bottom of the handbag. Cain turned up the radio and leaned back in his seat, smiling.

Jada gazed down at the sunny, peaceful ocean scene below. She shuddered. The piece of cold steel in her purse seemed even more frightening than a snake or a bomb. She realized it would soon confront her with a decision—and either choice she made could ruin her life either way.

Hate Crimes

For centuries—if not longer—individuals have been targets of violent acts just because they are different. They had done nothing wrong, except for being unlike another individual, yet someone felt that was reason enough to commit a violent act, hateful speech, or vandalism against these individuals or their property.

What is different about these individuals? In 1992, the U.S. Congress took up hate crimes, defining them as criminal acts committed in which "the defendant's conduct was motivated by hatred, **bias**, or prejudice, based on the actual or perceived race, color, religion, national origin, ethnicity, of another individual or group of individuals." Disabilities were added in 1994. In 2005, gender and sexual orientation were added to the list of protected groups. In addition to federal statutes, many states have their own laws, including sentencing guidelines, for hate crimes.

Hate crimes are also covered by Canadian federal law. According to their statutes, "a hate crime is committed to intimidate, harm or terrify not only a person, but an entire group of people to which the victim belongs. The victims are targeted for who they are, not because of anything they have done." Like U.S. law, the Canadian code also includes speech. Covered crimes include those based on color, race, religion, ethnic origin, or sexual orientation. Someone cannot be charged with a hate crime in Canada if the comments are true or if they are religious opinions.

In most cases, these statutes have not created new crimes. Instead, they allow the criminal justice system

Somewhere in America

- *Every hour someone commits a hate crime.*
- *Every day at least eight blacks, three whites, three gays, three Jews, and one Latino become hate crime victims.*
- *Every week a cross is burned.*

(Source: www.tolerance.org)

to increase sentences for those convicted of these crimes. For example, someone who assaults another might receive a sentence of five years. However, if the assailant is found guilty of attacking a member of one of the protected groups, several years might be added to that sentence.

How prevalent are hate crimes? In the overall scheme of crime statistics, the numbers are not huge. According to the FBI, in 2004 there were 7,649 *reported* cases of bias-related crimes in the United States. The important word in that sentence is reported. Many experts believe that many more instances go unreported because of fear or even embarrassment.

In 2004, California reported the most cases of bias-related crimes with 1,393, most based on race. With two reported cases, Mississippi had the fewest; they were both racially motivated as well.

Race and sexual orientation are the two most-cited reasons behind hate crimes. However, they are not the only precipitating factors. Of 520 hate crimes reported in New York State in 2004, 173 were religion based. The victim's race, ethnicity, and sexual orientation were the reasons behind the violence in the remaining cases.

Not everyone is in favor of classifying certain crimes as hate crimes. To them, doing so makes one person's life more valuable than another, just because they belong to a particular group. Some opponents of hate crime laws point out that they are just another way to separate one group of people from another. Although the intention might be good, it's still singling out a group of people for special treatment.

What do you think?

Chapter 6
You Wouldn't Dare

s soon as Nancy Torres heard the pounding on her office door, she knew who had come to see her. "Come in, Coach Steele."

The door flew open, and the coach entered the counselor's office, his face red. He strode up to her desk and demanded, "How dare you get my best player suspended, just before the Compton game? Do you realize what this might do for our school?"

Torres stayed calm. "Actually, Coach Steele, it was our principal who made the decision to suspend Cain Williams, not me. If you have problems with that decision, his office is just down the hall."

"Knock it off," snarled the coach. "You and I both know you started this thing. You got all sniffly over that loser, Jason Hughes, and then you took it out on my boy."

"Speaking of Jason Hughes," Nancy replied, "I'm glad you stopped by. I have some concerns—and I've been meaning to ask you about them."

"Concerns? What the heck are you talking about?"

"Jason says he went to you and reported how Williams was harassing him in PE class. He claims you told him not to say anything more, because Cain is your top player and any allegations against him would hurt the basketball team."

Steele's nostrils flared. "Rubbish. You know what a nut case Hughes is. I can't believe you're taking anything he says seriously."

She raised one eyebrow. "Mr. Steele, I decided to talk to you before going to the administration with this one—I felt that was the decent thing to do—but I want you to know, you will probably need to explain your actions again, soon."

The coach leaned over her desk, so that his face was close to hers. "Are you threatening me, Mrs. Torres?"

"No, I'm just telling you what I heard, and what I'm going to tell the principal. So if what you say is true, you should have nothing to be afraid of."

"You wouldn't dare."

"Oh?"

Steele leaned even closer; she could smell his cologne. "Listen here, lady," he growled, "I've been at this school for two decades. I've outlasted most everyone on the faculty. If you think you can make trouble for me, think again. I have lots of friends—with more pull than you have." He paused, and an unpleasant smile crossed his face. "Go ahead, make your complaint—and you'll wish you'd never set foot in Shore View High."

She returned his gaze and answered in a level voice, "Mr. Steele, I thought I was dealing with one bully—but it appears there are two."

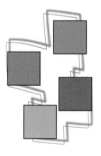

What Makes a Bully?

Violence is a learned behavior. Children learn it from their parents, from older siblings, from the school setting, and from television.

Violence and Family Influence

Parents or other primary caregivers are the first, and generally remain, the major influences on a child. It generally follows, then, that the family has a major influence on whether the child becomes aggressive. According to the Web site The ABCs of Bullying (pathwayscourses.samhsa.gov), these familial factors include:

- substance or alcohol abuse by someone in the family
- certain kinds of parenting behaviors toward the child
- family violence
- lack of warmth and involvement on the part of the parents
- overly permissive parenting
- lack of setting clear limits for the child
- lack of or inadequate parental supervision
- harsh, **corporal punishment**
- child maltreatment, such as sexual or physical abuse

According to the U.S. Department of Juvenile Justice, children who experience—as a victim of or witness to—violence have an increased risk of becoming violent themselves, committing crimes at a younger age, and are arrested more frequently than those who do not experience violence.

Some parents and caregivers do not take children's aggressive behavior seriously. While they may not actively condone these actions, their failure to stop such behaviors may indicate to the child that it is all right to be aggressive and to bully others.

As mentioned earlier, low self-esteem can be a factor in the development of aggression and bullying behavior in children. How parents treat children is a major player in the development of self-esteem. Parents who belittle their children, or who show a

Bullying sometimes has a racial element that stems from prejudice and fear.

lack of affection and involvement may be telling their offspring that they have no value; their place in the world—or in the family—is not important. Although perhaps less obvious, being overly permissive, not setting limits, and providing inadequate supervision all convey the same message. After all, you have to care about someone to care about what they do. Discipline is necessary, and it must be consistent; what was wrong this week should still be wrong next week.

Child abuse and excessive corporal punishment are not the same as discipline. With discipline, a child is being taught to replace an undesirable behavior with one that is acceptable. When harmful corporal punishment is used, the lesson becomes one of "might makes right." The only thing learned is that if you're big enough, it's all right to hit someone.

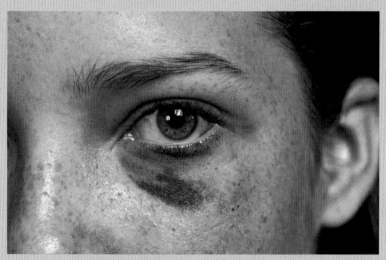

Child abuse tends to teach children that violence is an acceptable way to handle frustration and anger.

The cycle of child abuse has been well established for some time: the abusing parent was usually an abused child. But, the child may not wait until adulthood to continue the circle. What is the adult showing the child? Even if the parent tells the child that she shouldn't hit someone else, he's not practicing what he's preaching. Instead, the parent is showing that it's all right to hit—if you're the one with the power, in this case, the parent. The child may then go in search of someone over whom she has power. When found, the third party may become a victim of bullying and violence at the hands of the abused child. Sadly, this can begin another circle.

Violence and the Influence of Society and School

Next to family, the biggest influences on kids are school and peers—the individual's community. According to the Web site The ABCs of Bullying (pathwayscourses. samhsa.gov), societal and community factors that influence bullying and violence include:

- bigotry
- poverty
- easy access to alcohol and weapons
- poor schools
- the prevalence of violence in the media and popular culture

Violence and Schools

The role of the school is not to act as a parent. However, some of its responsibilities are similar.

Students should feel safe in their schools, both physically and psychologically. Weapons found in lockers and violence in schools (not necessarily their own) now means that many students are greeted each morning by security guards and metal detectors.

Though the guards and the metal detectors can help protect against some forms of violence, they are not a **panacea** for violence and bullying that still occur almost daily. The school must have a policy against violence and bullying, and like parents and discipline, it should be meted out consistently and fairly. Again, like the parent who shows his child how much he is valued through setting limits and teaching what is right and wrong, the school helps reinforce those self-esteem building tools.

Although there is no question that there is violence in school, it should be remembered that it is not as prevalent as one might think based on media coverage, especially when there is such an event as which occurred at Columbine High School in Colorado. In most cases, the violence faced by schools on an every day basis is more of the bullying variety.

Violence and the Media

Children and adolescents spend a *lot* of time watching television, going to movies, listening to music, and playing video or computer games. Violence contained in these forms of entertainment has not gone unnoticed by researchers and experts. However, not everyone agrees about how much influence the media has on violence. Some rush to blame heavy metal music when teens commit violent acts, especially school shootings. Others don't believe there is such a direct cause-and-effect relationship. However, a large body of evidence supports the relationship between viewing violent content on TV and engaging in aggressive behavior, as well as becoming desensitized to violence. According to the AAP policy statement on media violence, more that 3,500 research studies have examined the relationship between media violence and violent behavior and only eighteen found no influence.

Fast Fact

According to the Web site The ABCs of Bullying (pathwayscourses.samhsa.gov):

- **44 percent of the violent interactions on television involve perpetrators who have some attractive qualities.**
- **61 percent of television programs contain some violence, and only 4 percent of television programs with violent content feature an antiviolent theme.**
- **Nearly 75 percent of violent scenes on television feature no immediate punishment for or condemnation of violence.**

Regulating their children's exposure to violence is another parental responsibility. Watching television with their children and discussing what is viewed can help parents teach and reinforce the idea that the violence on television shows is not real—and consequences (if shown at all) may not be the same as they would be in the real world.

But what about violence on television that is real? Newscasts and documentaries often show graphic examples of violence; for some, the **axiom** "if it bleeds, it leads" still helps guide the content of their broadcasts. Again, this is an opportunity for parents

Unfortunately, the Internet has been used to spread damaging insults and rumors, spawning the birth of "Web bullies."

to view programs with their children and discuss their content and the context.

There are other ways that parents and caregivers can help monitor how much violence their children are exposed to in the media. Films, television shows, computer and video games, and music come with parental warning labels and ratings. Newer television sets, as well as most cable boxes, are equipped with V chips, which allow parents to block out certain programs because of language, violence, or sexual content.

The New Age of Bullying

When thinking about computers, the Internet, and violence, most people probably think about violent Web sites or computer games. However, with increasing access to the Internet because of cell phones and more widespread computer ownership, the Internet has become an increasingly popular bullying tool. Now, bullies don't need to rely on whispered rumors to spread gossip and lies. And, they're not geographically limited either. With a mouse click or the push of a cell phone button, untruths, gossip, and even photos—real or "doctored"—can be spread all over the world at one time.

Chapter 7

Everything Can Change in an Instant

Jada knew before Cain did that the moment of truth had come. They were walking onto the pier, headed for a soda at Sandy's Pier-End Café. *How weird*, Jada was thinking, *how we go through the motions as if everything is normal—when in fact Cain is crazy with anger, I'm scared stiff, and even the air feels like it's going to explode with tension.*

The sound of laughter was what alerted Jada to the approaching moment of crisis. The voices of a boy and a girl drifted upward from underneath the pier. Jada knew those voices—Vanna and Jason. A second later, Cain froze in mid-step, and his grip around Jada's waist tightened. Apparently he recognized the voices as well.

"It's the jerk. Him and that Chink slut."

Jada winced hearing the way he spoke about Vanna; *She's got a whole lot more sense and decency than you do,* she wanted to say—but she didn't dare utter the words.

Cain spoke quietly in her ear. "You got the piece?"

Jada shut her eyes. Her knees felt like rubber. She nodded.

"It's still loaded?"

"Haven't touched it."

Good. When I tell you, throw it to me."

He fastened a vice-like grip around her wrist and dragged her down the steps leading from the pier to the sand below.

Jason was leaning back against one of the enormous wooden supports, laughing. Vanna was in a bikini and sarong, smiling up at him. For an instant, they looked like the most innocent, happy pair in the world. *If only they knew what's coming,* Jada thought. She wanted to yell, "Run! Run for your lives," but she couldn't squeeze the words past her stiff lips.

"Hey!" Cain yelled at them.

They turned, and their laughter stopped.

"Dope-head," Cain snarled, "you ran crying to that counselor—got me in big trouble."

"Leave him alone!" Vanna cried.

Cain barely glanced at her. "Shut your trap. Stay out of this."

Vanna's eyes widened, and her fists clenched. Jada thought her face looked like it might burst with anger, but she held her jaws closed.

Cain turned back to Jason. "Some man you are, letting your little ho' defend you."

Jason stiffened. "Don't insult her."

Cain leered at Vanna. "Boat trash."

"Shut up!" Jason blurted.

"Make me."

Jason lunged. Swung. Missed.

Cain slapped him, a cat toying with a mouse.

Jason punched with his left; Cain blocked. . . .

WHOMP!

Cain looked startled as Vanna's purse slammed into his face. He looked even more surprised when Jason's third punch nailed him in the stomach. The star athlete doubled over and swore. Jada knew he'd never guessed two people he so despised could actually fight.

Cain shot a glance at Jada. "Now!" he screamed. "Throw it to me, now!"

WHAP! Vanna's purse left a red mark across Cain's face as she scored another hit.

"I mean it, Jada," Cain shouted.

Jada stood still.

Jason kicked Cain in the groin. "Take that, bully! How does it feel?"

Cain bent over, but he managed to straighten up and smash Jason in the nose. The thin boy put both hands over his face. Blood poured out. Vanna circled behind Cain and kicked him in the ribs. Cain turned in Jada's direction and leaped toward her.

"Gimme the gun. Now, you black slut!"

His last words wakened Jada from her frozen state. *What did he call me?*

"Give it to me now."

"What did you say?"

"*Now.*"

"*What* did you *call* me?"

Vanna delivered another kick to the ribs, and Cain struggled to inhale.

"You don't care about me. I'm—I'm just your toy." Jada's voice cracked.

Jason grabbed Cain from behind, but the bully thrust his elbow into Jason's ribs. The lighter boy fell onto the sand, grasping at his side and moaning. Vanna threw another kick at Cain's solar plexus. He grabbed her ankle and twisted it, throwing the girl face first onto the sand.

Cain's face was so twisted with rage that Jada barely recognized him. He lurched toward her and grabbed her arm, his nails cutting into her skin. "Give me that freakin' gun now, Jada, or I'm . . . gonna . . . kill you."

Jada looked into his eyes for a long moment. And then, very slowly, she reached into her bag.

She grabbed the pistol.

She pulled it out of her purse.

And then she threw with all her might.

Cain and Jada both stood still, their eyes glued to the shiny metal object, watching it arch up into the air, then out into the ocean, where it disappeared beneath the waves.

"You little—" Cain began, but he was interrupted by the piercing shrill of a lifeguard's whistle.

Three figures in bright orange sprinted toward them. Cain turned and dashed away beneath the pier, disappearing behind a nearby lemonade stand. Vanna and Jason stumbled toward the lifeguards, Jason holding his bleeding nose with one hand and his injured side with the other. Vanna whimpered and hobbled toward their rescuers. Jada scampered up the stairs back to the top of the pier.

Sometimes you do the right thing, and then you totally regret it, Jada mused.

She had freed herself from Cain's control. After months of compromise, fear, and shame, she had emerged into an altogether different world. She had made new friends in the process: Vanna, Jason, Josh, and Ashley seemed to realize that she was breaking away and needed the support of some fresh companions. She also found an ally in the school's counselor, Nancy Torres, who called Jada into her office the day after the incident under the pier "for a little chat." Ms. Torres was everything Jada hoped to be in the future—understanding, wise, and strong. Jada had found support in places she never expected.

And yet her life was a mess.

The cheerleading squad, formerly Jada's best friends at Shore View, became her tormenters. During practice, with the coach in the room, the girls acted like normal, but in the locker room or in class or the hallways, the squad insulted her, made snide comments, or simply pretended she didn't exist.

One day after practice, Jada approached Megan, her voice trembling. "Megan, please, just talk to me. Yell at me if you want to. Tell me off. Just talk to me, please?"

The other cheerleader finished tying her sneakers, stood up, and walked right *into* Jada, as if Jada were a vapor, as if she didn't even exist. Jada fell against a locker.

Jada gulped, and then she shut herself inside a toilet stall and sobbed, very quietly so the other girls wouldn't hear.

When Cain's suspension was over, he returned to school. Jason and Vanna filed a police report about the attack under the pier, but the pistol could not be found in the ocean, and Cain's parents filed a report countering the couple's claim, saying that Jason Hughes was a drug-crazed criminal who attacked their son. Jada was afraid she might soon be summoned to testify about the matter, a prospect she dreaded.

Cain's teammates added to Jada's tortures. Shawn, Cain's hulking henchman, had taken to sneaking up behind her in the hallway and blowing hot air on the back of her neck. He didn't say a word, but he scared the wits out of her.

Notes started appearing, slipped into Jada's backpack, stuffed in the louvers of her locker, or sometimes—frighteningly—placed in the pockets of her jacket. They were all anonymous, lewd, and threatening. Jada couldn't prove it, but she suspected that Bret, Cain's smaller and smarter accomplice, was the one writing them.

As for Cain, he kept his distance from Jada. With several threatened legal actions, a suspension, and the sharp eyes of Ms. Torres and the principal watching him, he knew better than to accost Jada in school. Instead, he would stand far away from her but in her line of sight, making obscene gestures. Sometimes, he would simply catch her eye from across the cafeteria and wink. Each time, Jada's blood ran cold.

This constant harassment seemed more than Jada could bear, but one day at lunch, she discovered that things could get even worse.

Eva Lucha, a junior cheerleader who fawned after Megan and the other seniors, pulled up a chair beside Jada in the cafeteria and flashed her a plastic smile. "Oh Jada, how does it feel to be a celebrity?"

"I don't know what you're talking about."

"Your Web site."

"But . . . I don't have a Web page."

"Oh, silly. Stop being modest. We know you do. *Every-one* knows you do. Why, your site is the hit of the whole school."

"You must be confusing me with. . ."

"Oh, no," Eva interrupted. "Why, look at this great picture I printed off this morning." She shoved a color photo in front of her.

Jada stared down at a brown-skinned, naked girl. Her own face had been digitally pasted onto the torso.

"That's not me!"

"Sure looks like you."

Jada gagged. "This is some sick joke."

"Really? I would never have guessed. Why, the journal entries seem so real."

"Journal entries?" Jada felt dizzy.

"Let me see, here's the one posted last night." Eva pulled another piece of printer paper out of her backpack and started reading it: "I want so bad to have sex again with Kyle Brown. . ."

"Kyle Brown?!" Jada shouted. "I've never had sex with Kyle!"

"But that's what you wrote." Eva's tones were sweet and innocent. "At least that's what it says in your journal posted on the Internet. Let's see, there's more." She continued reading. "I want to feel his hands all over my—"

"No!" Jada ripped the paper away from Eva, jumped up, and ran toward the cafeteria door. As she rushed past the table where the rest of the cheerleading squad was eating, Megan called after her, "Oh, Jada we were just saying what a *wonderful* Web site you have!"

Jada was too humiliated to tell her mother about the computer pages—but she had to tell someone. Finally, she went to talk with Ms. Torres, who got on the phone and threatened legal action if something wasn't done. Eventually, the site was removed—but it took two full weeks. More days than not, Jada stayed home from school, pretending to be sick. Truth was, she did feel sick—sick with shame, sick with embarrassment, sick with fear. What more could happen to her?

The managers of the popular site never did divulge who posted the images and fake journal. But Jada was sure she knew.

The campaign of humiliation might have continued indefinitely if fate had not intervened.

One night, Jada knew she had to get out of her house or she would explode, so she went window-shopping on Main

Street. Even in Southern California, winter evenings could be chilly, and Jada wore a faded leather jacket over her sweater. She stood on the sidewalk, looking at a cute outfit in the window of Mermaid Boutique. She could use more clothes, and she had her allowance money in her pocket, but she didn't feel like going in the store. *A few months ago, Cain would have bought me that.*

The thought brought no regret, only a sense of freedom. She sauntered back down the sidewalk toward the pier, her heart suddenly lighter. Maybe her life was hell—but at least she wasn't with Cain anymore.

Movement down a dark alley caught her attention. Afterward, she couldn't help but wonder: *What if I had kept going, not stopped and looked?*

But she did.

She could see two figures, both male. One was up against the wall; she could dimly make out a hand gripping his throat. The other figure was obviously threatening him. She couldn't be sure, but something about the second figure seemed familiar.

For a few moments, Jada was frozen with fear. What should she do? Ignore them, walk away? Was it really any of her business? Then she recalled a boy, slumped against the back wall of a restaurant, moaning after his attackers had torn his clothes, left him beaten and swollen. On that evening after the Covina game, Jada had looked straight ahead as she walked by. She had cast a quick guilty glance toward the injured boy and told herself, *I'm only an innocent bystander*, but her conscience had yelled back at her, condemning her. She hadn't felt the same about herself ever since.

But back then she was Cain's girl, an accessory to his brutality. Now, she had no excuse. And she didn't want one. She could no longer turn a blind eye.

She reached for her cell phone and then stopped as a uniformed policeman on a bicycle zipped right past her on the street. "Officer!" she shouted after him in her loudest cheering voice. "Hey! Officer! Someone needs help here!"

She couldn't see if the policeman heard her, because the next moment a sweaty hand clasped her mouth and then threw her onto the ground.

Jada stared up in the dim light saw. Cain's face was just inches from hers. She smelled the alcohol on his breath and knew he had been drinking. She felt as powerless now as she had that first day at the bus stop.

Click! Light from a far-off street lamp glistened along the line of a blade, and then she felt its chilly edge against her neck.

She inhaled, ready to yell, but his flat voice stopped her. "Well, babe, isn't this a surprise? Who'da thought my girl would come back to me?"

She sucked in another breath, but the knife's sharp edge suddenly stung against her.

"Looks like you want to scream, don't you? Get that cop's attention. But you wouldn't want to scar your pretty skin, would you?"

She held her breath, eyes wide with fear.

"Yell all you want. Do it. Before you get a sound out, I'll shove this blade right through your throat."

She kept her gaze fastened on his, but her hand moved slowly, slowly down into her purse.

"We had great times together, didn't we? But you had to ruin it. Can you believe, I chose you out of all the girls at Shore View—and you turned on me?" His hand moved away from her throat, and he waved the knife in the air, like some weird conductor.

Her fingers found a small plastic object, hidden in the interior of her handbag. She kept her eyes locked on Cain's face, let her lips quiver, holding his attention.

"You messed my whole life up. I don't know why I'm waiting. I should off ya right here. No one would know, no one would care."

Blinking, Jada looked into Cain's eyes and realized, *He's serious. Maybe he's too drunk to really know what he's doing. But he's going to kill me.*

Suddenly, a beam of light shot down the alley. "You there! Get away from her!"

She heard steps running toward them.

Cain whipped his arm back. He was going to swing the blade. . . .

F-F-S-S-S-T-T! She pressed hard on the tube of pepper spray, just inches from Cain's face.

He screamed and dropped the knife.

Then a blue figure hurtled out of the darkness and tackled Cain, wrestled the knife out of his grip, and cuffed him.

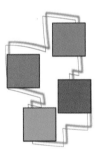

Violence and Substance Abuse

Most people have seen images of or heard stories of someone who becomes violent after having too much to drink. Many have also experienced this—as a victim or as the violent person—because this is a very real occurrence.

Drugs and alcohol can lessen a person's inhibitions, making that individual more open to acting in ways he wouldn't were he not under the influence of these substances. In children and youth, the drug of choice is most often alcohol, and there is a proven link between the use of alcohol and violence. According to the Web site The ABCs of Bullying (pathwayscourses. samhsa.gov):

- Forty percent of students who drank alcohol at school also carried a weapon at school,

Because alcohol lowers a person's inhibitions, it makes the risk of violence greater.

compared with 4.4 percent of those who did not drink.

- High school girls who smoke, drink, or use marijuana are more than twice as likely to report having been in a physical fight in the past 30 days as those who have never smoked, according to a study looking at the effects of substance abuse among girls and young women.

- Children who drink alcohol by the seventh grade are more likely to commit criminal and violent acts and have other problems, according to a **RAND** health study.

The same site goes on to list the following findings of an American Medical Association study comparing adolescent drinkers and nondrinkers. According to their findings, drinkers:

- scored lower on vocabulary, general information, memory, memory retrieval, and at least three other tests.

- experienced a 10 percent decrease in verbal and nonverbal information recall performance during a one-year period.

- showed "significant" *neuropsychological* deficits in youth between the ages of fifteen and sixteen with histories of extensive alcohol use.

- performed worse in school and were more likely to fall behind, and have an increased risk of social problems, depression, suicidal thoughts, and violence.

The adolescent doesn't have to be the one abusing alcohol or other substances to have it influence whether he will turn to violence. Having a parent or other family member who abuses alcohol may also increase the likelihood that a child or adolescent will become violent—or become a victim of violence. It's a well-known fact that children often mimic the behavior patterns of their parents and other influential people in their lives. When it comes to violence and substance abuse, this can be manifest in two ways: using alcohol and other substances and committing violent acts under their influence, and being abused at the hands of someone under the influence.

Perhaps less well known is how having a family member who abuses alcohol or other substances can make a child or adolescent an attractive target for bullying or teasing. This is especially true if the family member's substance abuse problem is publicly known.

Other Causes of Bullying

Sometimes bullying and aggressive behavior cannot be traced directly to exposure to violence. In some cases, it is caused by psychological disorders such as oppositional defiant disorder or conduct disorder.

Oppositional Defiant Disorder

Although aggression and bullying may be a part of oppositional defiant disorder (ODD), there is much more to this illness. Symptoms of ODD may include:

- frequent temper tantrums
- excessive arguing with adults

- active defiance and refusal to comply with adult requests and rules
- deliberate attempts to annoy or upset people
- blaming others for his or her mistakes or misbehaviors
- often being touchy or easily annoyed by others
- frequent anger or resentment
- mean and hateful talking when upset
- seeking revenge

For the individual with ODD, these symptoms interfere with day-to-day life.

A young person with oppositional defiant disorder (ODD) may deliberately upset others and then blame the other person for the conflict. She is easily annoyed, often feels resentment, and when she's upset, she may become insulting and hurtful.

Conduct Disorder

Conduct disorder refers to a group of behavioral and psychological problems, not just one. Individuals with conduct disorder may find it almost impossible to follow rules, and they persistently violate the rights of others and age-appropriate social values and norms. Someone with conduct disorder:

- bullies, threatens, or intimidates others
- initiates fights
- has used a weapon
- is physically cruel

Most teenagers quarrel occasionally, but an adolescent who physically bullies others and initiates fights may have a psychiatric disorder known as conduct disorder.

- steals from a victim while assaulting them
- forces someone into sexual activity
- deliberately engages in fire-setting to cause damage
- deliberately destroys others' property
- has broken into someone else's home, business, or car
- lies to obtain things or to avoid obligations
- shoplifts
- often stays out at night without parental consent
- runs away from home
- is truant

The individual with conduct disorder will likely exhibit some, but not all of those behaviors.

Because there is a possibility that someone who bullies or is violent in other ways may have a condition such as ODD or conduct disorder, it is important that they have a thorough examination, so that conditions like ODD or conduct disorder can be eliminated.

Chapter 8
Hard-Won Victory

How are you feeling today?"

Nancy Torres leaned over the desk toward the young woman in front of her. *She looks amazingly good after all she's been through,* thought the counselor.

Jada flashed a hint of a smile before answering. "Better than the day before, I think."

Torres nodded. "That's good."

"But a lot of the time, I still feel like crap."

"That's not surprising, Jada, after everything you've been through."

"Sometimes I still get afraid. I'll go to my locker, and I'll think Cain is behind me."

"That would be pretty hard for him to do, considering where he is now."

"Are you sure the county is going to keep him in there?"

"Given all the crimes Cain has been charged with, and the testimony of the officer who found you in the alley, the judge decided Cain should be tried as an adult. While he's waiting for his trial, he can't get out on bail. So he is going to be behind bars for a good while, even before sentencing."

Jada nodded, then stared out the window. Far away, the ocean's waves glittered in the sunlight. "I thought when I came to Shore View I'd start this wonderful new life," Jada said, "but instead, this was the year from hell."

"Have you thought of returning to your old school?"

"Yeah, my mom asked if I want to do that. I told her, 'No. Wherever I go, there I am. I can't escape the decisions I've made. So I might as well deal with my life here.'"

"Wise choice. Do you regret leaving the cheerleading squad?"

"No way. Those girls are so shallow and mean. I'm amazed I ever called them my friends." Jada kept her eyes on the distant water. "You know what the worst part of this whole thing is?"

"What?"

"I *chose* to be Cain's girlfriend. I didn't have to do it."

"You're too hard on yourself, Jada. Look at your peers. They're as influenced by others as you were. That's normal when you're an adolescent. Learning to be yourself, no matter what others think, is a hard lesson, one we've all had to learn. And besides, men like Cain have become experts at manipulation. When I was your age, I probably would have done the same thing."

"Really? You're not just saying that?"

"Yes, really. I did some pretty dumb stuff in high school." She smiled. "But I'm not at liberty to tell students about my shady past."

Jada grinned. "I'm not sure I'd want to go there anyway."

Jada's eyes returned to the window, and Nancy waited, sensing that the girl was searching for something important.

"Ms. Torres. . ."

"Yes?"

"I don't know how to thank you enough. If you hadn't gotten the principal to crack down on Cain. . ." She shuddered.

"It wasn't just me, Jada. You made some vital decisions. You took control of your life, and changed your destiny. When you threw that gun into the water, and when you yelled for help in the alley—you probably saved at least a couple of people's lives. You should feel proud of yourself."

"Thanks. But I can't imagine what 'proud' feels like right now. I'm so full of messed-up emotions." She sighed, and turned back toward the counselor. "I hear Mr. Steele left the school."

"Yes, he decided this would be a good time to take early retirement."

"I don't suppose you had anything to do with that?"

"Like I said, he chose now to retire." Nancy knew she couldn't say more than that, so she changed the subject. "How are you doing in your classes, Jada?"

"Doing all right, Mrs. Torres. I'm getting B's and C's."

"That's pretty good, everything considered. Have you thought about what you'll do after graduation?"

"Yeah, I'm gonna go to Huntington Beach Community College for the next two years, and pull my grades up to get into Cal State."

"Excellent. And do you have some thoughts about your future career?"

"Yes." Jada's voice was shy. "I want to study psychology . . . maybe become a school counselor."

"Well, I'm not going to disagree with that choice. Although it can be a challenging career." Nancy smiled. "So tell me, when you're a counselor, what kind of advice will you give to a young woman who's being harassed by a domineering but popular boy?"

Jada looked back at the counselor, her eyes bright, her mouth curved upward with the satisfaction born from hard-won victory. "I'd tell her not to give in—that she can do better than that. Maybe she'd listen to me, maybe not. But if not, I hope I can be there for her, to help her pick up the pieces. The way you were for me."

The bell rang, and Jada jumped to her feet. "I've gotta run—test in biology class today."

"Good luck, Jada."

"Thanks, Ms. Torres." She picked up her book bag and disappeared out the door.

If Jada stays on this course, Nancy Torres thought, *some lucky high school is going to have an outstanding counselor.*

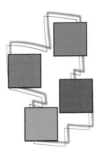

The Costs of Bullying

Bullying isn't an innocent part of growing up. According to the Web site www.nobully.com, bullying's effects are widespread, and even those not directly involved in bullying suffer its consequences:

For the targets, who often endure their school years in a more or less permanent state of anxiety, the effects include not only the cuts, bruises and wounding of physical assaults. Physical, verbal and relational bullying can all result in reluctance to go to school, repeated headaches and stomach pains, bed-wetting, poor appetite, anxiety, irritability, aggression and depression. Bullying is a direct attack on a student's status and sense of belonging to their peer group and often results in low self-esteem. In the most extreme cases targets have taken out their anger through school shootings or by committing suicide.

Students who habitually bully miss the opportunity to learn an alternative to aggression. Research tells us that they often develop a habitual tendency to abuse power. Approximately 25 percent of school bullies will be convicted of a criminal offense in their adult years.

The students on the sidelines (the "bystanders") commonly report extreme discomfort at witnessing bullying, but say that they do not know how to prevent it. They are silenced by their fear that bullies will target them if they speak out. Often they grow up believing that they are powerless to stop abusive behaviors in others.

For the school, the effects are time wasted in tackling a problem that is resistant to change, absenteeism, compromised student academic performance, low teacher morale, negative perceptions of the school by the wider community, and increasing parent

A young bully sometimes grows up to be an older bully! About a quarter of these young people who cannot control their tempers will commit criminal offenses as adults.

hostility. The school campus becomes a place where diversity is unvalued and unprotected. Schools are increasingly subject to litigation for failing to provide a safe learning environment and in some cases are being held responsible for the suicides and school shootings by students targeted by bullies.

In other words, allowing bullying to continue creates a situation in which no one—bully, victim, or bystander—can achieve their best and prepare for a fulfilling life.

Bullying damages both the victim and the aggressor.

And Bullying Doesn't Stop at Schools

It would be nice to think that bullying stops when one leaves school, but that isn't always the case. Workplace bullying is a very real problem that organizations such as the Workplace Bullying Institute are trying to stop.

The organization, active in both the United States and Canada, defines workplace bullying as the "repeated, health-harming mistreatment of one or more persons (the targets) by one or more perpetrators that takes one or more of the following forms:

- verbal abuse

- threatening, humiliating or offensive behavior/actions

- work interference—sabotage—which prevents work from getting done."

In many ways, workplace bullying is identical to that which occurs at school: it's based on getting power over someone else, others are drawn into choosing sides (or being made to feel as they must choose sides or become a target themselves), and the workers' goals are undermined by bullying—just as students' quest to learn can be circumvented by the actions of bullies.

According to a 2000 study by the Workplace Bullying Institute, one in six U.S. workers had directly experienced workplace bullying during the previous year. More women than men were targets of bullying (80 percent). Women were also the primary bullies (58 percent). Seventy-one percent of the bullies were bosses.

Despite legislation proposed by the Workplace Bullying Institute and others, there are few legal ramifications to bullying on the job. Organizations such as the Workplace Bullying Institute continue to work to stop bullying and provide a safe work environment for employees.

A Permanent Solution to Bullying

In 2005, in a small town in Manitoba, Canada, sixteen-year-old Gary Hansen took pride in the twenty-year-old snowmobile he had worked hard to restore. Not everyone saw it as a **laudable** accomplishment though, and Gary found himself bearing the brunt of a bully who teased him about how it looked. This wasn't Gary's first experience with bullying. Earlier in his academic career, his parents had kept him out of school for two years because he had been the target of bullying. In 2005, Gary was back in school, and things seemed to be going well—until the snowmobile brought bullying back into his life. But, the harassment didn't end with the snowmobile's looks; the bullies also harassed him about his sexuality.

In 2005, Gary Hansen hanged himself.

Fourteen-year-old Dawn-Marie Wesley of British Columbia, Canada, was the target of constant bullying by three classmates. She knew she should get help, but, as she wrote in her suicide note, " 'If I ratted they would get suspended and there would be no stopping them'" (CBC News, www.cbc.ca/printablestory.jsp).

In 2000, Dawn-Marie Wesley hanged herself.

School had always been difficult for Jared High of Washington State. But, during middle school, Jared became the target for a well-known bully, who brutally assaulted him in the school gymnasium. He also fell victim to cyber bullying. Just after his thirteenth birthday, in September 1998, Jared had taken all he could stand.

On September 29, 1998, Jared High shot himself, with his father on the phone with him.

It's not just suicides and teenagers.

In 1998, ten-year-old Myles Neuts slowly strangled to death as he hung from a coat hook in an elementary school in Ontario, Canada. Bullies had placed him on the hook in the restroom and brought friends in to watch him. Finally, one of the onlookers told a teacher. It was too late for Myles, though, who died four days later.

Isn't suicide a bit extreme—even if you are the target of bullying? Definitely, but imagine being someone who is taunted, ridiculed, perhaps even hit day after day after day after day after . . .

According to the American Academy of Child and Adolescent Psychiatry, adolescents are at an increased risk of suicidal thoughts and actions if they are the targets of bullies. In one study, it was found that among the bullied and even the bullies, 43 percent had experienced suicidal thoughts; 8 percent had attempted suicide in the eight months between the study and the follow-up. Some psychologists have even coined a term for the phenomenon—bullycide.

As discussed elsewhere in this book, people who are the targets of bullies often become depressed, and sadly, those who might be able to help often miss the signs of depression and suicidal **ideation**. The National Suicide Prevention Lifeline (www. suicidepreventionlifeline.org) lists the followings as signs that someone is considering suicide:

- threatening to hurt or kill oneself or talking about wanting to hurt or kill oneself
- looking for ways to kill oneself by seeking access to firearms, pills, or other means
- talking or writing about death, dying, or suicide when their actions are out of the ordinary for the person

People sometimes turn to suicide when they feel they have no other options. Teenagers who are the targets of bullies are more apt to feel that their life has become a one-way journey that leads only to their deaths. They do not realize there are always alternatives.

- feeling hopeless
- feeling rage or uncontrolled anger or seeking revenge
- acting reckless or engaging in risky activities—seemingly without thinking
- feeling trapped—like there's no way out
- increasing alcohol or drug use
- withdrawing from friends, family, and society
- feeling anxious, agitated, or unable to sleep—or sleeping all the time
- experiencing dramatic mood changes
- giving away possessions
- seeing no reason for living or having no sense of purpose in life

If you experience any of these signs—or you know someone who does—get help immediately. The National Suicide Prevention Lifeline has trained experts available 24/7, just a phone call away: 1-800-273-TALK.

Treating Bullies—and the Bullied

As bleak as statistics may make the future for the person who bullies and the target sound, there is hope. But, as with most illnesses and behavior issues, the sooner the problem is recognized and treatment begun, the better the outlook for success.

The first step in treating the individual who exhibits violent or bullying behaviors is to check for physical causes or for conditions such as ODD or conduct disorder. They have their own treatment criteria.

For the child who does not have those conditions, treatment will necessarily involve both the family and the school. Remember that the family is the primary source of behavior patterning for children. In many cases, the bully is repeating actions he has seen or experienced at home. The goal of treatment is to teach the bully that such actions are not acceptable

Bullying and other forms of violence are serious problems in today's world. They require treatment at both the individual and the societal levels.

options for dealing with any type of situation. This will require the cooperation of the family, and that could be the most difficult step of all. Everyone needs to be made aware of the outlook for individuals who do not change their bullying behavior patterns. The individual, the family, and the therapist/counselor must be willing to commit to a possibly lengthy period of intense work.

Bullying and other forms of violence are most likely to take place in schools where such behavior is accepted or tolerated, or ones in which punishments are given **arbitrarily** rather than consistently. According to the National Youth Violence Prevention Resource Center, when there is a schoolwide commitment to stop violent behavior—including bullying—occurrences can be reduced up to 50 percent. The center reports that one approach that has proven to be successful involves:

- raising awareness about bullying,
- increasing teacher and parent involvement and supervision,
- forming clear rules and strong social norms against bullying, and
- providing support and protection for all students.

Everyone is involved in the process and agree to get involved in curbing the problem. There is no more "looking the other way"; instead, everyone looks toward the problem, thereby helping to find the solution.

It would be easy to believe that once bullying stops, the target of the behavior would be fine—you pull the splinter and the pain goes away. Unfortunately, dealing with a human being who has been belittled, harassed, and perhaps physically assaulted is much more difficult than pulling out a splinter. A school counselor or other mental health–care professional can help the formerly targeted individual regain her self-esteem, self-confidence, and sense of safety and security.

What You Can Do if You Are Being Bullied

1. Talk to your parents or an adult you can trust.

2. It's not useful to blame yourself for a bully's actions. But, do not retaliate or let the bully see how much you've been upset by his or her actions or words.

3. Act confident—you're less likely to be the target of a bully.

4. Try to make friends with other students, as bullies are more likely to leave you alone if you are in a group.

5. Do not resort to violence or carry a weapon. Carrying weapons can make a difficult situation deadly and increase the chances that you will be harmed. Violence (or the threat of violence) doesn't solve violent situations.

(*Source:* Adapted from National Youth Violence Prevention Resource Center. www.safeyouth.org)

Glossary

~~~~~~

antisocial: Indifferent to the comfort or needs of others; uncomfortable with the company of others.

arbitrarily: Done in a random way.

axiom: A statement or idea that people accept as self-evidently true.

bias: An unfair preference for or dislike of something or someone.

condone: To regard something that is considered wrong in a tolerant way, without criticizing it or feeling strongly about it.

corporal punishment: The striking of a person's body as punishment.

covert: Hidden; not obvious.

ideation: The formation of ideas.

incessant: Continuing without interruption.

innuendo: An indirect remark or gesture that usually carries a suggestion of impropriety.

laudable: Admirable and worthy of praise.

neuropsychological: Pertaining to a branch of psychology that studies how behavior and emotions are linked to physical aspects of the brain and nervous system.

panacea: A supposed cure for all diseases or problems.

pervades: Spreads throughout an area.

RAND: A nonprofit research organization.

truancy: Staying out of school without permission.

variables: Things capable of change.

Further Reading

Dellasega, Cheryl, and Charisse Nixon. *Girl Wars: 12 Strategies That Will End Female Bullying*. New York: Simon and Schuster, 2003.

Elliott, Michelle. *Bullying*. London: Hodder, 2005.

Field, Evelyn. *Bully Busting: How to Help Children with Teasing and Bullying*. Lane Cove, New South Wales, Australia: Finch, 2003.

Kalman, Izzy. *Bullies to Buddies: How to Turn Your Enemies Into Friends*. Staten Island, N.Y.: Wisdom Pages, 2005.

Shore, Kenneth. *The ABC's of Bullying Prevention*. Port Chester, N.Y.: Dude Publishing, 2005.

Simmons, Rachel. *Odd Girl Speaks Out: Girls Write About Bullies, Cliques, Popularity, and Jealousy*. Orlando, Fla.: Harcourt, 2004.

Slavens, Elaine. *Bullying: Deal With It Before Push Comes to Shove*. Halifax, Nova Scotia, Canada: Lorimer, 2003.

Winkler, Kathleen. *Bullying: How to Deal With Taunting, Teasing, and Tormenting*. Berkeley Heights, N.J.: Enslow, 2005.

For More Information

ABCs of Bullying
pathwayscourses.samhsa.gov

American Academy of Pediatrics
www.AAP.org

Bully Police USA
www.bullypolice.org/Brenda.html

National Youth Violence Prevention Resource Center
www.safeyouth.org

NYU Child Study Center
www.aboutourkids.org

Stop Bullying Now
stopbullyingnow.hrsa.gov

The Story of Jared High
www.JaredStory.com

Students Against Violence Everywhere (SAVE)
www.nationalsave.org

Teaching Tolerance
www.tolerance.org

Teen Health
www.kidshealth.com

Publisher's note:
The Web sites listed on this page were active at the time of publication. The publisher is not responsible for Web sites that have changed their addresses or discontinued operation since the date of publication. The publisher will review and update the Web-site list upon each reprint.

Bibliography

Barry, Tammy, and John E. Lochman. "Aggression in Adolescents: Strategies for Parents and Educators." http://www.nasponline.org.

Dill, Karen E., and Craig A. Anderson. "Violent Video Games Can Increase Aggression." *Selfhelp Magazine*, 2000. http://www.selfhelpmagazine.com.

"FBI Reports Increase in Hate Crimes." *ABC News*, November 26, 2004.

Foltz-Gray, Dorothy. "The Bully Trap." http://www.tolerance.org/teach/magazine/features.jsp?p=0&is=12&ar=95&pa=4.

"Girls and Bullying." http://www.ncpc.org/parents/Girls_and_Bullying.php.

"Hate-Crime Laws Face Challenges." *Intelligence Report*. http://www.splcenter.org.

"Put a Stop to Bullying Behavior." http://www.TeenGrowth.com.

Rust, Michael. "Researchers Seek Causes of Teen Violence." United Press International, 2001.

"Violence Leads to Violence." http://www.fcusas.com/Violence.html.

"What Is a Hate Crime?" *CBC News*. http://www.cbc.ca/news/background/hatecrimes.

"What Should Parents and Teachers Know About Bullying?" http://www.focusas.com/Bullying.html.

Winerman, L. "Among Teens, Aggression Equals Popularity." *Monitor of Psychology* 35(June 2004).

Zuckerman, Diana. "What Is to Blame for Youth Violence? The Media, Guns, Parenting, Poverty, Bad Programs, Or . . ." http://jerz.setonhill.edu/weblog/permalink.jsp?id=901.

Index

Picture Credits

iStockphoto: pp. 34, 75, 96, 110, 117
      Blazic, Ana: p. 80
      Damkier, Mikael: p. 31
      Horrocks, Justin: p. 76
      McEntire, Brian: p. 22
      Perkins, Thomas: p. 109
      Pruitt, Jim: p. 99
      Schmidt, Chris: p. 59
      Szota, Michal: p. 115
Jupiter Images: pp. 21, 46, 57, 100

To the best knowledge of the publisher, all other images are in the public domain. If any image has been inadvertently uncredited, please notify Harding House Publishing Service, Vestal, New York 13850, so that rectification can be made for future printings.

Authors

Kenneth McIntosh is a freelance writer living in northern Arizona with his family. He has written two dozen educational books, and taught at junior high, high school, and community college levels.

Ida Walker is a graduate of the University of Northern Iowa in Cedar Falls and did graduate work at Syracuse University. The author of several nonfiction books for middle-grade and young-adult readers, she currently resides in upstate New York.

Series Consultants

Dr. Bridgemohan is an Assistant Professor in Pediatrics at Harvard Medical School and is a Board Certified Developmental-Behavioral Pediatrician on staff in the Developmental Medicine Center at Children's Hospital, Boston. She specializes in assessment and treatment of autism and developmental disorders in young children. Her clinical practice includes children and youth with autism, developmental language disorders, global delays, mental retardation, attentional and learning disorders, anxiety, and depression. Dr. Bridgemohan is Co-director of residency training in Child Development at Children's Hospital, Boston, and is co-editor of "Bright Futures Case Studies for Primary Care Clinicians: Child Development and Behavior," a curriculum used nationwide in Pediatric Residency training programs. Dr. Bridgemohan has also published research and review articles on resident education, toilet training, autism screening, and medical evaluation of children with developmental disorders.

Cindy Croft, M.A.Ed., is the Director of the Center for Inclusive Child Care (CICC) at Concordia University, St. Paul, MN. The CICC is a comprehensive resource network for promoting and supporting inclusive early childhood and school-age programs and providers with Project EXCEPTIONAL training and consultation, and other resources at www.inclusivechildcare. org. In addition to working with the CICC, Ms. Croft is on the faculty at Concordia University and Minneapolis Community and Technical College.